1/2017

TABLETOP WARS
SURPRISE THE ENEMY
Make Your Own Traps and Triggers

Thanks to the creative team:
Senior Editor: Alice Peebles
Fact checking: Kate Mitchell
Design: www.collaborate.agency

Hungry Tomato™
A division of Lerner Publishing Group, Inc.
241 First Avenue North
Minneapolis, MN 55401 USA

For reading levels and more information, look up
this title at www.lernerbooks.com.

Main body text set in Bodoni 72.
Typeface provided by International Typeface Corp.

Library of Congress Cataloging-in-Publication Data

Names: Ives, Rob, author. | De Quay, John Paul, illustrator.
Title: Surprise the enemy : make your own traps and triggers / Rob
Ives ; illustrated by John Paul de Quay.
Description: Minneapolis : Hungry Tomato, [2016] | Series:
Tabletop wars | Audience: Ages 8–12. | Audience: Grades 4 to 6. |
Includes index.
Identifiers: LCCN 2016012042 (print) | LCCN 2016020013
(ebook) | ISBN 9781512406375 (lb : alk. paper) | ISBN
9781512411706 (pb : alk. paper) | ISBN 9781512409246 (eb pdf)
Subjects: LCSH: Booby traps–Juvenile literature. | Weapons–
Juvenile literature. | Military art and science–Juvenile literature.
Classification: LCC UF860 .I94 2016 (print) | LCC UF860
(ebook) | DDC 623.4/514–dc23

LC record available at https://lccn.loc.gov/2016012042

Manufactured in the United States of America
1-39310-21147-5/11/2016

TABLETOP WARS
SURPRISE THE ENEMY
Make Your Own Traps and Triggers

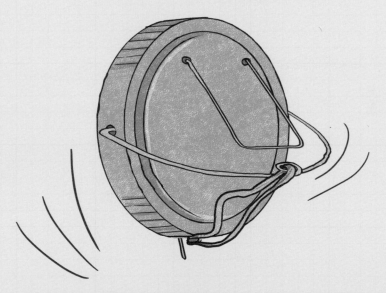

by Rob Ives

Illustrated by John Paul de Quay

HUNGRY TOMATO™

Minneapolis

Safety First!

Take care and use good sense when making these miniature traps and triggers. Even though the models are small, and you may use soft missiles with the models made in other books in this series, the unexpected can happen. Be responsible and always be safe.

Bolts, darts, and other missiles can cause damage when fired with force. Never aim anything at people, animals, or anything of value.

Look for the safety warning sign in the activities and ask an adult for assistance when you are cutting materials.

Watch for this sign throughout the book. You may need help from an adult to complete these tasks.

CONTENTS

TRAPS AND TRIGGERS

This book shows you how to make small, fun models of devices that have been used to trip up and trap the enemy throughout history. These of course will only result in cries of surprise, not injury—and, hopefully, amusement.

Supply List:

To make the traps and triggers in this book, you will need these supplies. Most items can be found at home, school, or a craft store:

Thick and Thin Corrugated Cardboard

Wooden Craft Sticks

Ballpoint Pen

Aluminum Foil

Strong Cardboard Tube, 1.7 inches (4.5 cm) wide

Felt-tip Pens

Pencils

Paper

Magazine Pages

Plastic Cable Ties

Plastic Bottle Top, 1.7 inches (4.5 cm) wide

Pipe Cleaners

Large and Small Rubber Bands

Long Paper Clips, 2 inches (5 cm)

Mini Marshmallows

Small, Empty Matchbox

Tiny Traps

This is a fun guide to making simple miniature traps from everyday items. The devices that inspired them come from different historic times and places—one is even prehistoric! They have a common trigger mechanism that delivers an instant burst of marshmallows or just surprise!

So, delve into your drawers and cabinets for the few items you will need, and exercise your fingers and brain. The projects can be made in multiples, too, so they are great to make with friends. And remember, before you start, read the safety information on page 4, and look out for the safety warning sign where you'll need a little adult help. So get ready, get set, and see your traps jump!

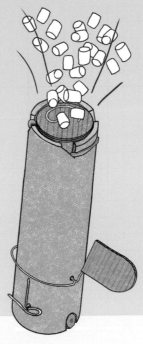

TIPS

Some projects need pencils to be cut into sections. Do ask for help with this. An efficient way to do this is to cut each face of the pencil in turn, and then snap it apart. Tidy up any unevenness with a knife.

Also ask for help with cutting the barrel of a pen—this can be quite tricky! One way of doing it neatly is to use a file to cut a notch all the way around, and then snap off the piece. Also make sure to cut things on a cutting mat.

With adult help, use the sharp end of a pencil or a craft drill to make small holes in cardboard. Use pliers to straighten out paper clips.

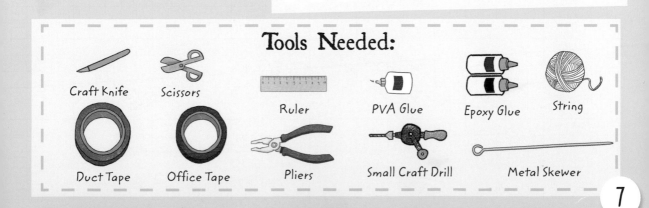

Tools Needed:

Craft Knife   Scissors   Ruler   PVA Glue   Epoxy Glue   String

Duct Tape   Office Tape   Pliers   Small Craft Drill   Metal Skewer

FINGER TRAP

Defend your desk from invading forces by laying several finger traps in your territory. The design has "jaws" with jagged duct tape "teeth" that won't dent your foes' digits—but will make them proceed with caution.

Supplies:

Plastic Cable Ties x 4

Long Paper Clips x 5

Rubber Bands x 2 (one large, one small)

Thin Corrugated Cardboard (small piece)

Pencils x 3 (one cut short)

Ballpoint Pen

Wooden Craft Sticks x 3

Felt-tip Pen

Tools:

Ruler

Duct Tape

Craft Knife

Scissors

Pliers

Epoxy Glue

PVA Glue

Instructions
STAGE 1

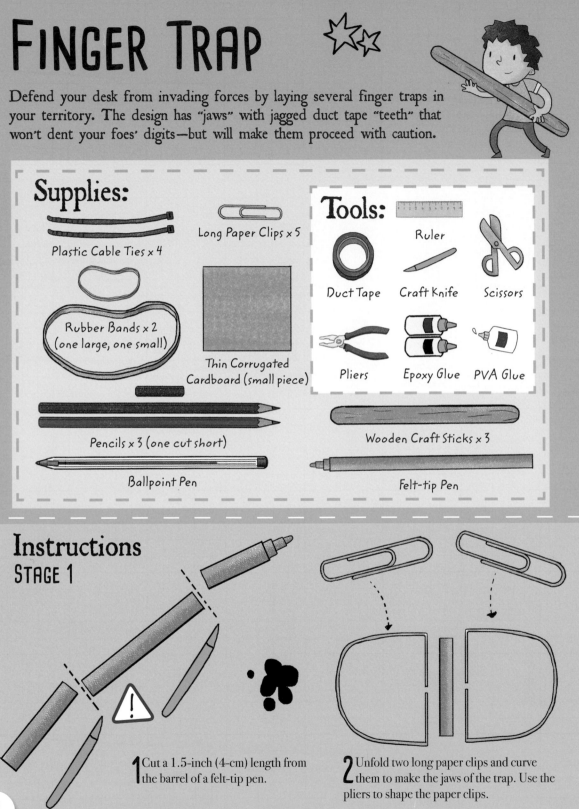

1 Cut a 1.5-inch (4-cm) length from the barrel of a felt-tip pen.

2 Unfold two long paper clips and curve them to make the jaws of the trap. Use the pliers to shape the paper clips.

STAGE 2

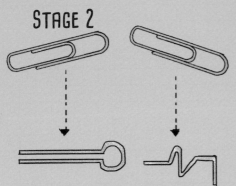

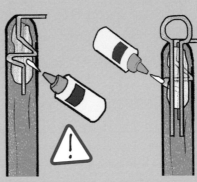

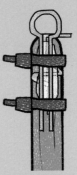

3 The spring that closes the jaws is made from two craft sticks and two paper clips bent to shape (as above). Cut the two craft sticks to 3.5 inches (9 cm) long and glue them back-to-back.

4 Glue one paper clip to the end of the craft sticks with epoxy glue. This will act as the hook for the trigger.

5 Glue the other paper clip on top with epoxy glue.

6 Hold the paper clips down with cable ties. Trim the ends.

STAGE 3

7 Cut a piece of ballpoint pen inner tube 0.7–1.2 inch (2–3 cm) long. Cut a 1.2-inch (3-cm) length of pencil to act as a pivot.

8 Glue the felt-tip pen barrel and ballpoint pen inner tube with epoxy glue to the pencils 0.7 inch (2 cm) from the ends. Tie on with cable ties and trim. Glue the pencil piece crosswise about 1 inch (2.5 cm) from the pen barrel. This is the pivot.

9 Slip the ends of the jaws through the loop on the end of the spring piece. Fit the jaws into the pen barrel.

10 Hold the spring piece on the pivot with a small rubber band. Wrap a large rubber band around two or three times near the pencil points to make the spring piece springy.

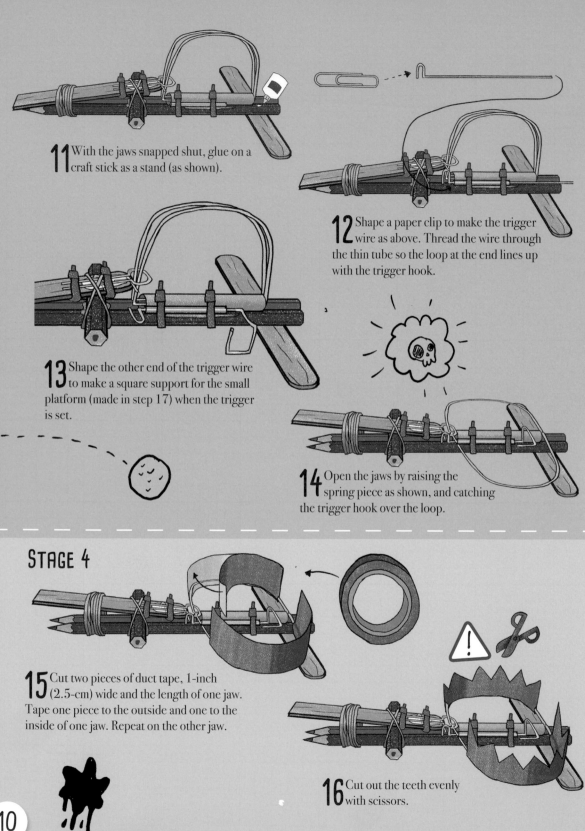

11 With the jaws snapped shut, glue on a craft stick as a stand (as shown).

12 Shape a paper clip to make the trigger wire as above. Thread the wire through the thin tube so the loop at the end lines up with the trigger hook.

13 Shape the other end of the trigger wire to make a square support for the small platform (made in step 17) when the trigger is set.

14 Open the jaws by raising the spring piece as shown, and catching the trigger hook over the loop.

STAGE 4

15 Cut two pieces of duct tape, 1-inch (2.5-cm) wide and the length of one jaw. Tape one piece to the outside and one to the inside of one jaw. Repeat on the other jaw.

16 Cut out the teeth evenly with scissors.

17 Tape a small cardboard disc, roughly 1.5-inch (4-cm) wide, to the trap platform. Now wait for an unsuspecting person's finger to land!

Ouch!

THE MANTRAP

In the eighteenth century, poor workers would sneak on to rich people's land to steal a rabbit or pigeon for dinner. These estates had traps set up that grabbed a person's leg in metal jaws when they were accidentally stepped on. There was no way out—the trap could not be pulled apart. It was only opened with a key.

WHIRLING HELICOPTERS

Surprise your friends with these whirling helicopters. The design comes from plants that send out flying seeds. Leonardo da Vinci imagined the first full-size version of a helicopter. See how far yours can fly!

Supplies:

Paper

Wooden Craft Sticks (one per helicopter)

Magazine Pages

Aluminum Foil

Tools:

Scissors

PVA Glue

Ruler

Instructions
STAGE 1

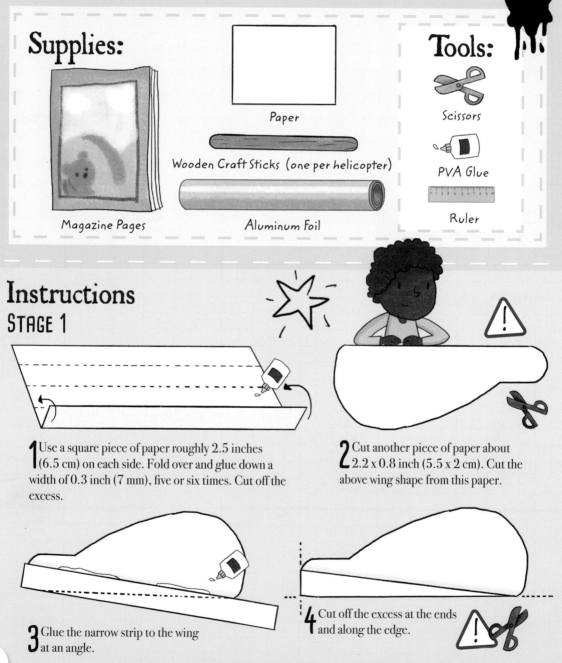

1 Use a square piece of paper roughly 2.5 inches (6.5 cm) on each side. Fold over and glue down a width of 0.3 inch (7 mm), five or six times. Cut off the excess.

2 Cut another piece of paper about 2.2 x 0.8 inch (5.5 x 2 cm). Cut the above wing shape from this paper.

3 Glue the narrow strip to the wing at an angle.

4 Cut off the excess at the ends and along the edge.

STAGE 2

5 Cut off the two ends of a craft stick with sharp scissors.

6 Glue the craft stick ends to the wing.

STAGE 3 (OPTIONS)

7 Instead of using plain white paper as described in step 2. Make colorful helicopters from magazine pages.

8 Make more wings from aluminum foil. Throw them in the air and watch them . . .

Fly!

LEONARDO'S HELICOPTER

The earliest design for a full-size helicopter came from the brain and pen of artist Leonardo da Vinci in 1493. Of course, the engine had not yet been invented. His idea was to have men on a circular platform turning a central spindle to make the "sails" rotate and provide liftoff. This could not have happened due to the weight of the machine—but Leonardo's idea was centuries ahead of its time (as usual).

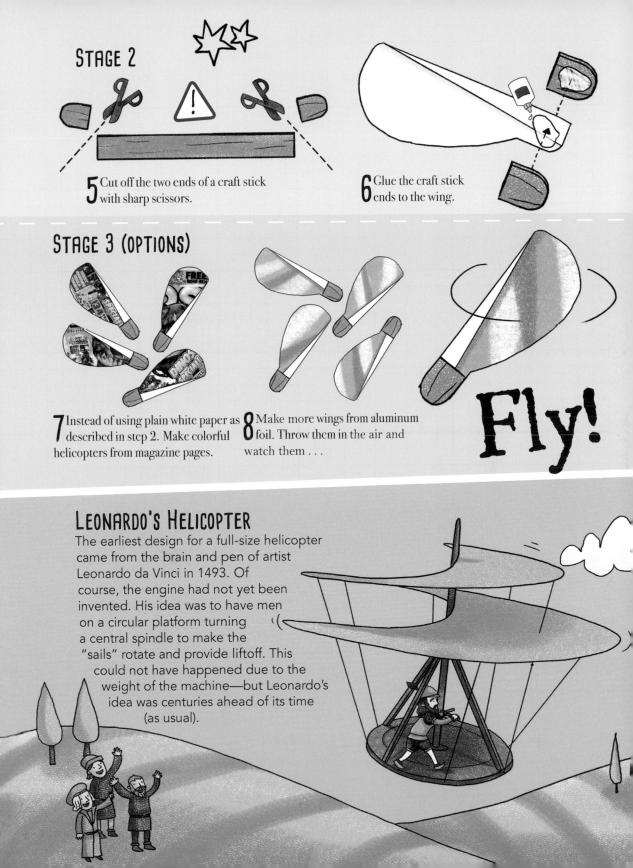

Book Trap

It's said that clever traps were laid to stop robbers from ever reaching the treasures in Egyptian tombs. You too can make your target jump the very next time they open a book or take a drink.

Supplies:

Small Rubber Band

Long Paper Clip

Corrugated Cardboard

Tools:

Office Tape

Scissors

Pliers

Instructions

STAGE 1

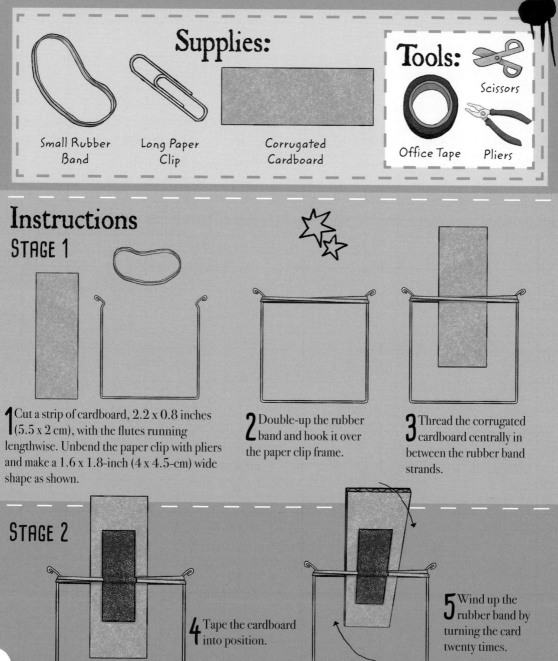

1 Cut a strip of cardboard, 2.2 x 0.8 inches (5.5 x 2 cm), with the flutes running lengthwise. Unbend the paper clip with pliers and make a 1.6 x 1.8-inch (4 x 4.5-cm) wide shape as shown.

2 Double-up the rubber band and hook it over the paper clip frame.

3 Thread the corrugated cardboard centrally in between the rubber band strands.

STAGE 2

4 Tape the cardboard into position.

5 Wind up the rubber band by turning the card twenty times.

STAGE 3

Aah!

6 Place the trap inside a book, close the book, . . .

7 . . . and wait for someone to open it!

8 You can also try hiding it under someone's mug!

TOMB TRAPS

The ancient Egyptians had many ways of protecting the riches buried with a pharaoh. They placed heavy stones over doorways and attached them to tripwires. The stones came crashing down if an intruder stepped on the wire. Poisonous powders might also be released into the air in a similar way.

SPIDERBOX

Boi-oing! Open the matchbox and out springs a spider. Keep it in your pocket for use at a moment's notice to make your friends jump—just when they least expect it. Don't worry though—it's only a nice fluffy spider!

Supplies:

Small Rubber Band

Small, Empty Matchbox

Pencil

Corrugated Cardboard

Pipe Cleaner

Tools:

Craft Knife

PVA Glue

Instructions
STAGE 1

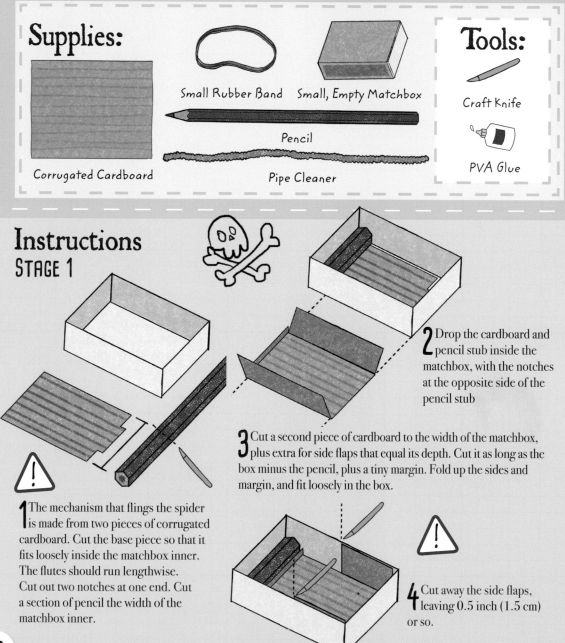

2 Drop the cardboard and pencil stub inside the matchbox, with the notches at the opposite side of the pencil stub

3 Cut a second piece of cardboard to the width of the matchbox, plus extra for side flaps that equal its depth. Cut it as long as the box minus the pencil, plus a tiny margin. Fold up the sides and margin, and fit loosely in the box.

1 The mechanism that flings the spider is made from two pieces of corrugated cardboard. Cut the base piece so that it fits loosely inside the matchbox inner. The flutes should run lengthwise. Cut out two notches at one end. Cut a section of pencil the width of the matchbox inner.

4 Cut away the side flaps, leaving 0.5 inch (1.5 cm) or so.

5 Remove the cardboard from the matchbox. Then cut two notches in the upper piece (as shown).

6 Cut and glue on a smaller piece with a flap, to cover two-thirds of the upper. This will keep the spider in place.

STAGE 2

7 Thread the rubber band around the tab on the base piece, then underneath and over the pencil.

8 Fit the upper piece on top, threading the rubber band around the flaps and inside the notches.

9 Place the mechanism inside the matchbox.

10 Slide on the matchbox outer as far as the flaps.

STAGE 3

11 Cut a pipe cleaner into four equal lengths.

12 Twist the lengths around each other at the center.

13 Curve the "legs" to make a spider shape.

STAGE 4

14 Load the box with the spider on the launch platform.

15 Tuck the platform down, close the box and . . .

18

3,2,1... Open!

STONE AGE ANIMAL TRAP

It would seem impossible for a very large animal to be caught in a box. But tens of thousands of years ago, an effective way of hunting was to dig a huge pit in the ground and cover it with branches. Early hunters then drove an animal so near the trap that it fell in, and there was no escape. Elk, moose, reindeer, and bears were all caught in this way.

Finger Trigger

Had enough surprises? Why not demonstrate this in front of an audience? This trap springs into action with a simple trigger mechanism. Just the touch of a finger makes it jump.

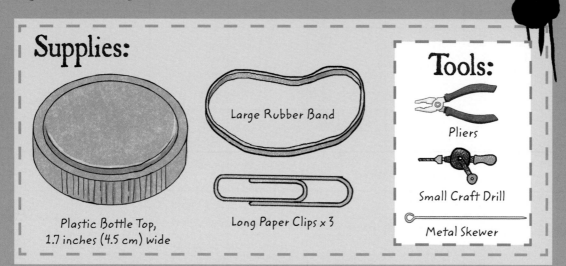

Supplies:

Plastic Bottle Top, 1.7 inches (4.5 cm) wide

Large Rubber Band

Long Paper Clips x 3

Tools:

Pliers

Small Craft Drill

Metal Skewer

Instructions
STAGE 1

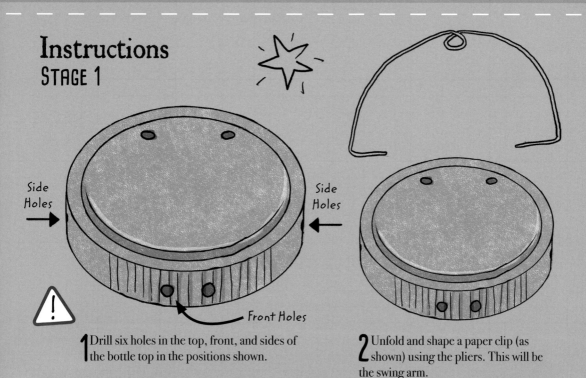

Side Holes

Side Holes

Front Holes

1 Drill six holes in the top, front, and sides of the bottle top in the positions shown.

2 Unfold and shape a paper clip (as shown) using the pliers. This will be the swing arm.

3 Thread the rubber band into one of the two holes at the front of the bottle top and catch it in place (as shown).

4 Thread the other end of the rubber band into the loop in the swing arm.

5 Fit the swing arm into the two side holes.

STAGE 2

6 Straighten another paper clip to make the trigger pin. Bend one end into a loop. The pin can be too long, as it will be cut down later.

7 Straighten another paper clip to make the trigger arm. Form one end into a loop, and bend a right angle near the loop.

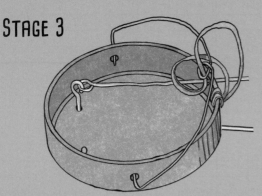

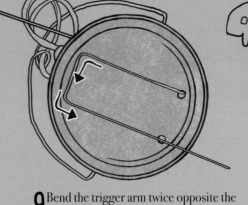

8 Slot together the loops on the trigger pin and arm. Close up the loops so they can't pull apart. Thread the trigger pin out through the hole next to the rubber band. Thread the trigger arm through one of the holes in the top.

9 Bend the trigger arm twice opposite the two holes in the top, and at about the same distance apart.

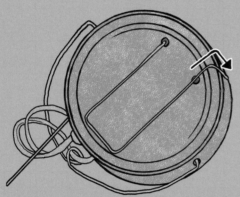

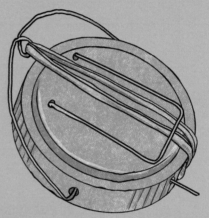

10 Make a third bend in the arm so it will fit down through the second hole on the bottle top. Move the swing arm to the side of the bottle top with the holes.

11 Trim the trigger arm to length and thread it into place through the second hole. Make sure it lies over the rubber band as shown.

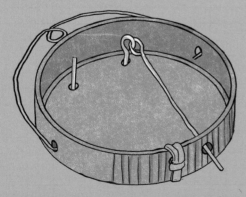

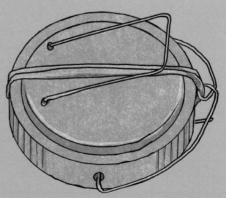

12 This is how it looks on the underside.

13 Move the swing arm all the way around, then lift the trigger arm so that the trigger pin just catches the swing arm. Trim the trigger pin to length.

14 Touch the trigger arm and the trap jumps!

Boing!

NINJA TRAPS

Ninja knew all about tripwire traps. They even had clever ploys for keeping safe while asleep. They stretched a rope from the door of their room and attached it to a bucket at their bedside. The bucket was filled with pebbles. If an enemy opened the door, the rope tipped the bucket over with a mighty clatter, waking the ninja and startling the enemy.

MARSHMALLOW TRIGGER

Get your supplies of marshmallow shrapnel or soft candies ready. Make a cool launch mechanism, load it, and keep it in a discreet place, then when your foe comes by you'll be doing them a favor—a marshmallow bombardment!

Supplies:

Corrugated Cardboard

Small Rubber Bands x 2, 2.7 inches (7 cm)

Mini Marshmallows

Strong Cardboard Tube, 1.7 inches (4.5 cm) wide

Long Paper Clips x 3

Pencil

Tools:

String

Office Tape

Small Craft Drill

Pliers

Craft Knife

Ruler

PVA Glue

Metal Skewer

Instructions
STAGE 1

7 inches (17 cm)

1.7 inches (4.5 cm)

1 Cut the tube to 7 inches (17 cm) in length

2 Cut four notches in one end of the tube as shown. These will be the lugs that the rubber bands hook over in step 20. This end is the top.

3 At the other end of the tube, cut two notches to fit a pencil snugly. The pencil should line up with the straight-sided lugs at the other end (see step 2).

1.7 inches (4.5 cm)

4 Cut a section of the pencil to the same length as the diameter of the tube.

STAGE 2

5 Drill three holes in the tube as shown. The hole nearest the edge is halfway between the other two.

1.4 inches (3.5 cm)

0.6 inch (1.5 cm)

6 Shape this "crow's foot" trigger piece from a paper clip.

7 Fit it into the side hole on the tube with the long piece running up the outside toward the top.

8 Bend one of the trigger wires into a horizontal loop (as shown).

9 Shape the trigger retainer (left) from another paper clip.

10 Fit the trigger retainer into the holes as shown. With the trigger retainer horizontal, trim off the trigger upright so that it is just hooked under the retainer.

STAGE 3

Trigger upright hooked under the retainer

11 Cut a vane from a piece of corrugated cardboard, with the flutes running vertically as shown.

1.2 inches (3 cm)

2 inches (5 cm)

12 Thread the long end of the trigger retainer into one of the flutes in the vane.

13 Cut a piece of corrugated cardboard for the piston. Roll it around a pencil to curve it.

2.4 inches (6 cm)

6 inches (15 cm)

14 Roll up the piston so it is a loose fit inside the tube. Tape it closed with office tape.

15 Cut four evenly spaced notches in the base of the piston to make lugs.

16 Thread a rubber band into the lugs on each side and tape in place.

STAGE 4

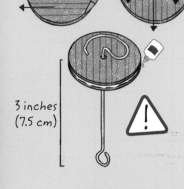

17 Use the top of the piston as a guide to cut out two cardboard discs. Glue them together with the flutes at right angles. Shape a trigger hook from a paper clip (as shown left). Make a hole in the center of the piston top and thread in the trigger hook.

3 inches (7.5 cm)

18 Glue the piston top in place and let the glue dry completely (refer to the bottle's instructions).

19 Make a hole in each side of the piston halfway down with a pencil point.

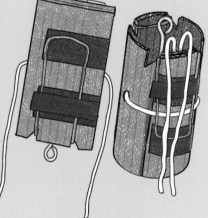

20 Cut some string roughly twice the length of the outer tube. Thread it through the holes on the piston and out through the base. The picture on the left shows the piston with the base at the top.

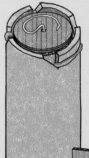

21 Drop the piston into the top of the tube, hooking the rubber bands over the lugs. Pull the strings so that the top of the piston lines up with the top of the tube.

22 Glue the pencil stump into the slots in the base, then tie the string around the pencil so that the piston stays lined up.

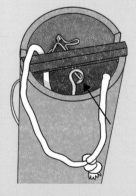

23 Pull the string to lower the piston. Thread the trigger into the hook.

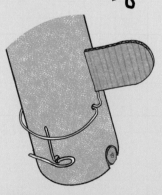

24 Hold the trigger against the side of the tube and lower the trigger retainer into place.

25 Fill the tube with marshmallow shrapnel and twist the vane down . . .

Stand clear! Boom!

GRAVE TRAPS

In the eighteenth century, people used to rob graves at night and sell the bodies to medical students so they could study human anatomy. It was so common, that people set up traps in cemeteries to frighten off grave robbers. A grave trap consisted of a gun set on a block of wood. The gun was hidden in the graveyard, and the trigger attached to wires. A robber who stepped on a wire set off the gun.

THE FINISHED MODELS

These amazing models spring into action at just the touch of a finger. The element of surprise is what matters!

Finger Trap

Based On: Mantrap

Invented In: The seventeenth century

Purpose: To deter poachers

Whirling Helicopters

Helicopter Invented By: Leonardo da Vinci

First Practical Helicopter Design: VS-300, successfully tested in 1940

Book Trap

Based On: Tomb Trap

Invented By: Ancient Egyptians

Purpose: To deter robbers

Spiderbox

Based On: Stone Age animal trap

Construction: Camouflaged pit

Purpose: To catch animals for food and clothing

Marshmallow Trigger

Based On: Eighteenth-century grave trap

Purpose: To deter grave robbers

Operated By: Tripwire

Finger Trigger

Based On: Ninja trap

Purpose: To expose enemy movements

Operated By: Tripwire

Traps and Triggers in History

The trigger mechanism has been used to operate all kinds of traps from early times. Helicopters are also an amazingly early invention, but had to wait until the modern age to take off!

Beware of Traps

All kinds of traps were used to deter trespassers from gardens and estates in eighteenth and nineteenth-century Britain, and also in the United States. Mantraps snapped their teeth shut on a person's leg when touched, and could inflict severe injuries. Spring guns fired when a trespasser stepped on an attached wire. They could cause death as well as injury.

An estate owner had to make it known that these contraptions had been laid. If they did not, they were responsible for any injury that occurred. Sometimes the guns were accidentally triggered by a property owner's servants and gamekeepers—and by the owner—with dire results.

Leonardo's Flying Machines

The first helicopter design came from China at least 1,700 years ago. But it was simply a toy called the Chinese top. It had a propeller set on a spindle wrapped with string. When the string was pulled, the toy rose in the air.

Who knows—perhaps Leonardo da Vinci saw one of these toys. He certainly drew the first helicopter design. It measured 15 feet (4.5 m) across, and was essentially a large screw with a winglike rotor, which compressed air as it turned to produce flight. Today's helicopters work in a similar way. Da Vinci recommended that, if it were ever built (which it wasn't), the helicopter should be tested over water to avoid a crash landing!

The ever-inventive da Vinci also came up with an ornithopter, a human-powered flying device. The pilot would lie face down in the center of the machine and pedal a crank to make two large wings flap. There were also hand cranks to give extra power. For this, as for many of his aviation ideas, da Vinci studied the flight and behavior of birds and bats.

INDEX

THE AUTHOR

Rob Ives is a United Kingdom-based designer and paper engineer.
He began making cardboard models as a math and science teacher,
and then was asked to create two books of models. His published
titles include *Paper Models that Rock!* and *Paper Automata*. He
specializes in paper animations and projects, and often visits schools
to talk about design technology and demonstrate his models.

THE ARTIST

John Paul de Quay is an illustrator with a BSc in Biology from
the University of Sussex, United Kingdom, and a postgraduate
certificate in animation from the University of the West of England.
He devotes his spare time to growing chili peppers, perfecting his
plan for a sustainable future, and caring for a small plastic dinosaur.
He has three pet squid that live in the bath, which makes drawing in
ink quite economical . . .